Pennies, Nickels, and Dimes

Penny 1¢   **1 cent**

When we count **pennies**, we count by **ones**.

Nickel 5¢   **5 cents**

When we count **nickels**, we count by **fives**.

Dime 10¢   **10 cents**

When we count **dimes**, we count by **tens**.

Count the coins. Write the amount on the line.

1.

 1   2   3   _____ _____ _____ _____   ¢

2.

 5   10   15   _____ _____ _____   ¢

3.

 10   20   _____ _____ _____   ¢

Count On to Find the Amount

Count on to find the total amount.
Write the amount on the line.

"Count by tens and then by fives."

| 10 | 20 | 25 | 30 | 35 | 35¢ |

1.

_____ ¢

2.

_____ ¢

3.

_____ ¢

4.

_____ ¢

2 Counting On with Two Types of Coins

Can You Count These Coins?

What is the price of each toy?
Count the money. Write the total amount on the tag.

| 10 | 20 | 25 | 26 | 27 | 28 |

1.

2.

3.

4.

Counting Pennies, Nickels, and Dimes

Count the money in each purse.
Write the amount on the line.

1. 10 ¢

2. _____ ¢

3. _____ ¢

4. _____ ¢

5. _____ ¢

6. _____ ¢

Match the Amounts

Count the money in each purse.
Write the amount on the line.
Match the amount with the item.

1. 36 ¢

33¢

53¢

2. _____ ¢

GLUE 36¢

3. _____ ¢

61¢

4. _____ ¢

5. _____ ¢

30¢

46¢

6. _____ ¢

How Much Is a Quarter?

1 quarter = 25¢   **2** dimes and **1** nickel = 25¢   **5** nickels = 25¢

Count the money in each group.
Write the amount on the line.
Cross out the group not equal to a quarter.

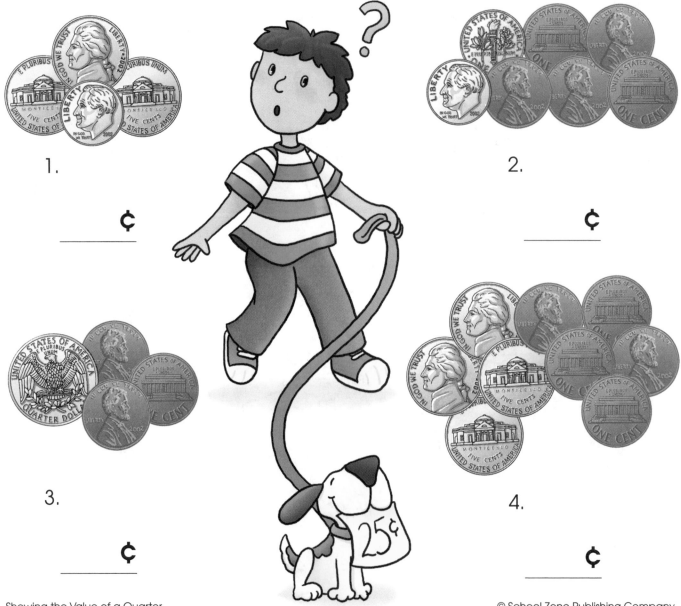

1.

_____ ¢

2.

_____ ¢

3.

_____ ¢

4.

_____ ¢

More Quarters

25¢

50¢   75¢

How much does each item cost?
Write the amount on the price tag.

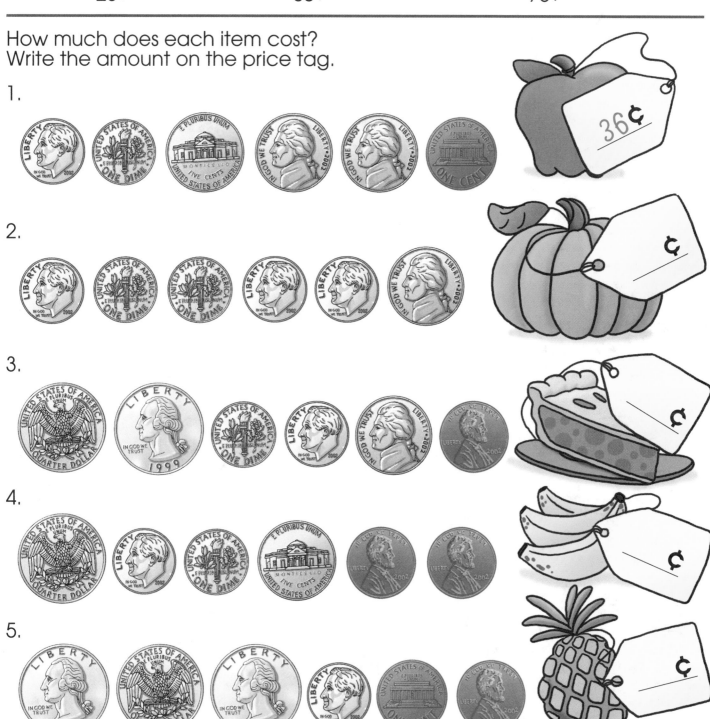

1.

36¢

2.

¢

3.

¢

4.

¢

5.

¢

Is There Enough?

Count the money. Is there enough money to pay for the item?

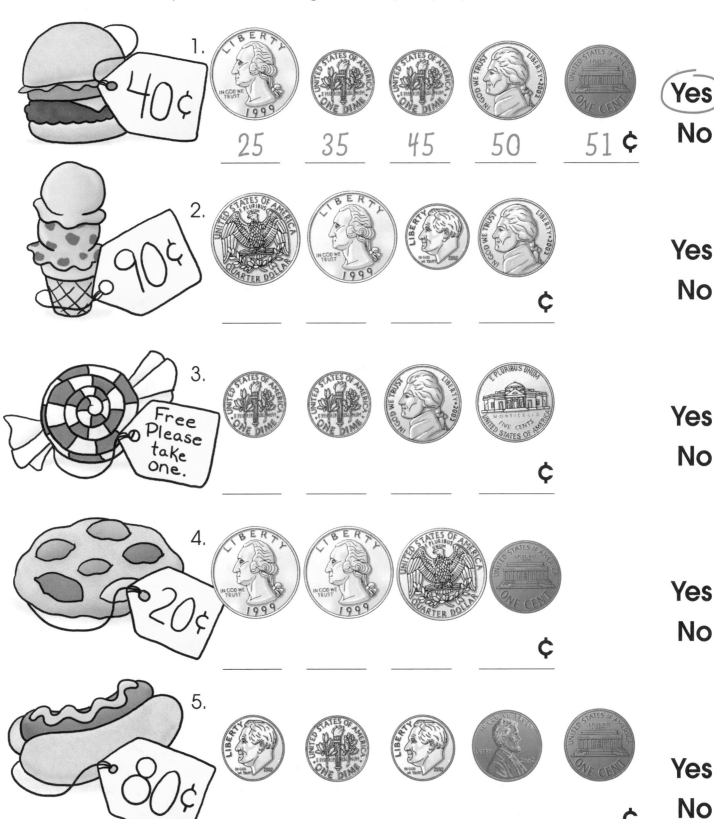

1. 25 35 45 50 51 ¢   Yes No

2. _____ ¢   Yes No

3. _____ ¢   Yes No

4. _____ ¢   Yes No

5. _____ _____ _____ _____ ¢   Yes No

Pick Coins to Buy a Flower

Circle the coins you will need to buy a flower.

1. 38¢

2. 46¢

3. 70¢

4. 61¢

5. 52¢

6. 87¢

How Much Is a Half Dollar?

"Or 50 pennies"

Half Dollar = 50¢   **2** quarters = 50¢   **5** dimes = 50¢   **10** nickels = 50¢

Circle the coins in each group to show 50¢.

1.

2.

3.

4.

Showing the Value of a Half Dollar

Find Banks with 50¢

Count the money in each bank. Write the amount on the line.
Circle each amount that is equal to 50¢.

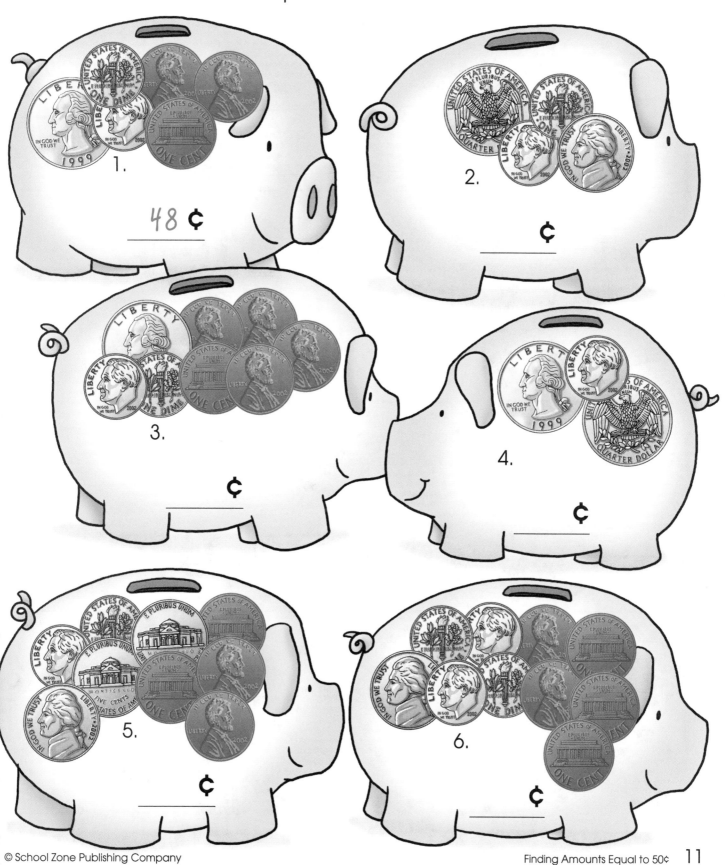

1. 48 ¢

2. _____ ¢

3. _____ ¢

4. _____ ¢

5. _____ ¢

6. _____ ¢

Which One Costs More?

Count the money. Write the amount on the line.
Circle the item that costs more.

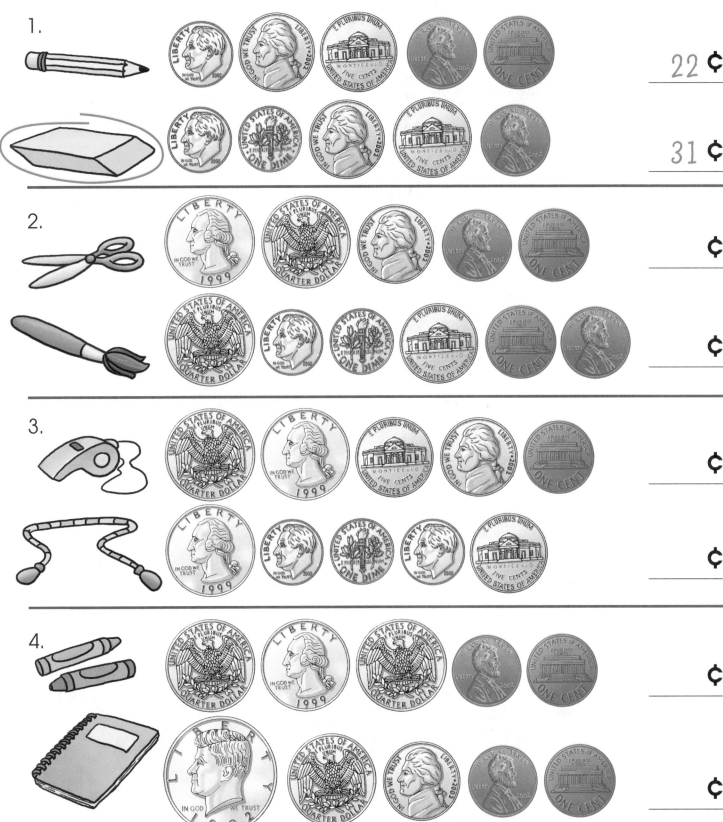

1. _____ 22 ¢

_____ 31 ¢

2. _____ ¢

_____ ¢

3. _____ ¢

_____ ¢

4. _____ ¢

_____ ¢

Which Amount Is Less?

Look at the two ways to show money.
Write the amount for each way.
Circle the amount that is less.

1.

   25 ¢   (20 ¢)

2.

   ___ ¢   ___ ¢

3.

   ___ ¢   ___ ¢

4.

   ___ ¢   ___ ¢

5.

   ___ ¢   ___ ¢

6.

   ___ ¢   ___ ¢

7.

   ___ ¢   ___ ¢

8.

   ___ ¢   ___ ¢

Which Coins Are Missing?

Count the money. Look at the amount.
Draw the fewest missing coins.

Watch out! There may be more
circles than coins needed.

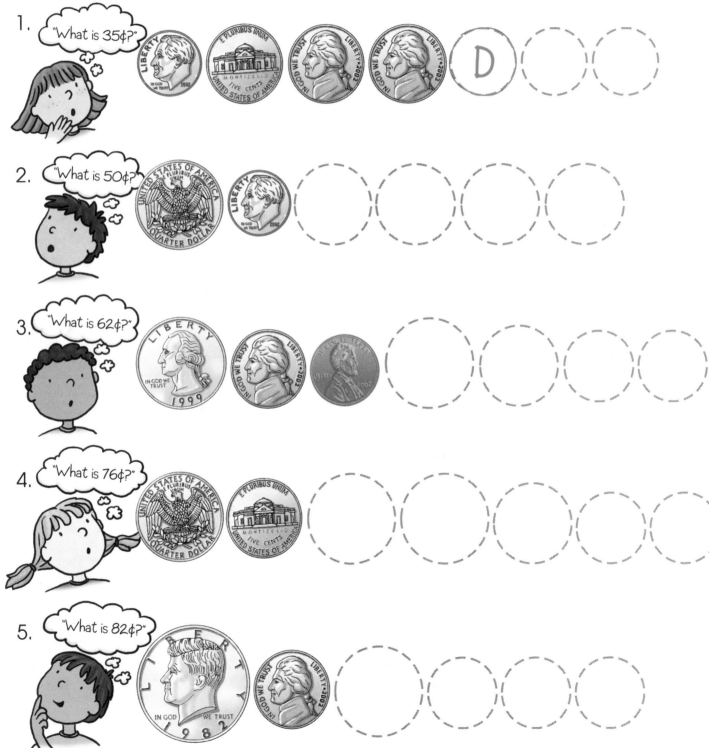

1. "What is 35¢?"

2. "What is 50¢?"

3. "What is 62¢?"

4. "What is 76¢?"

5. "What is 82¢?"

Pay for It with Coins

Look at the price of each item.
Draw the fewest coins to pay for it.

Draw Q for quarter.
Draw D for dime.
Draw N for nickel.
Draw P for penny.

1. 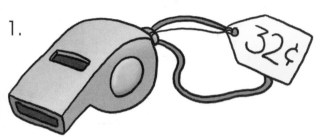 32¢

2.  28¢

3.  45¢

4.  56¢

5. 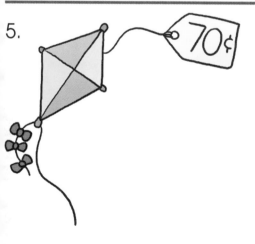 70¢

6.  98¢

Shopping at the Store

How much does each item cost?
What is the total cost of 2 items?

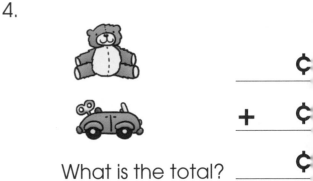

1.

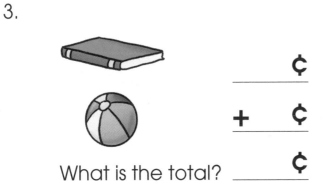

$$\begin{array}{r} 39\ \text{¢} \\ +\ 28\ \text{¢} \\ \hline \end{array}$$

What is the total? __67__ ¢

2.

$$\begin{array}{r} \text{¢} \\ +\ \text{¢} \\ \hline \text{¢} \end{array}$$

What is the total? _____

3.

$$\begin{array}{r} \text{¢} \\ +\ \text{¢} \\ \hline \text{¢} \end{array}$$

What is the total? _____ ¢

4.

$$\begin{array}{r} \text{¢} \\ +\ \text{¢} \\ \hline \text{¢} \end{array}$$

What is the total? _____ ¢

5.

$$\begin{array}{r} \text{¢} \\ +\ \text{¢} \\ \hline \text{¢} \end{array}$$

What is the total? _____ ¢

6.

$$\begin{array}{r} \text{¢} \\ +\ \text{¢} \\ \hline \text{¢} \end{array}$$

What is the total? _____

What's Your Change?

Find the amount of change.
Write the amount.
Draw the coins.

Have	Buy	Change
1.	30¢	N 35 ¢ − 30 ¢ 5 ¢
2.	37¢	¢ − ¢ ¢
3.	35¢	¢ − ¢ ¢
4.	69¢	¢ − ¢ ¢
5.	79¢	¢ − ¢ ¢

How Many Coins Do You Need?

Write the number of coins to make the amount using fewest coins.

53¢	1				3
27¢					
18¢					
69¢					
76¢					
37¢					
92¢					

Make each amount using more coins.

53¢			5		3
27¢					
18¢					
69¢					
76¢					
37¢					
92¢					

Money Crossword Puzzle

Write the amounts in the puzzle.

Across

a. **6** dimes

b. **4** dimes and **2** pennies

c. **1** half dollar and **9** nickels

d. **6** nickels

e. **1** quarter

f. **1** dime and **5** pennies

g. **1** dollar

h. **2** quarters

i. **3** quarters

j. **3** quarters, **1** nickel, and **4** pennies

Down

a. **6** dimes and **2** pennies

b. **9** nickels

c. **1** half dollar and **4** dimes

d. **3** dimes and **5** pennies

e. **5** nickels

f. **10** pennies

g. **2** nickels

h. **5** dimes and **5** pennies

i. **7** dimes and **4** pennies

j. **1** half dollar, **1** quarter, **1** dime, and **4** pennies

Hour Time

A clock has two hands. The short hand shows the hour.
When the long hand points to **12**, we say **o'clock**.

hour hand

minute hand

The hour hand points to **2**.
The time is **2 o'clock**, or **2:00**.

Read the hour hand first. Then read the minute hand.
Write the time in two ways.

1.

___2___ o'clock

__2__ : __00__

2.

_____ o'clock

_____ : _____

3.

_____ o'clock

_____ : _____

4.

_____ o'clock

_____ : _____

5.

_____ o'clock

_____ : _____

6.

_____ o'clock

_____ : _____

Show Hour Time

Draw hands on the clock face to show the time.
Write the time on the digital clock.

1. **5 o'clock**

2. **10 o'clock**

3. **6 o'clock**

4. **12 o'clock**

5. **3 o'clock**

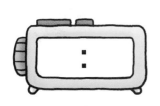

6. **8 o'clock**

Minutes in an Hour

It takes the minute hand **5** minutes to move from one number to the next.

Count the minutes by **5**s.
Write the minutes on each line.

How many minutes in an hour? _____

How Many Minutes?

Look at the clock. Find the numbers
1 to 60 around the clock face.

1. Circle these numbers: **15 30 45 60**

1.

2. Start at 12. Count around the clock face
   by 5s for the yellow part.

   _5_ , _10_ , _____

   How many minutes in this part of the clock?

   _____ minutes

2.

3. Start at 12. Count around the clock face
   by 5s for the yellow part.

   _5_ , _____ , _____ , _____ , _____ , _____

   How many minutes in this part of the clock?

   _____ minutes

3.

4. Start at 12. Count around the clock face
   by 5s for the yellow part.

   _5_ , _____ , _____ , _____ , _____

   _____ , _____ , _____ , _____

   How many minutes in this part of the clock?

   _____ minutes

4.

Half Past the Hour

The long hand tells the minutes. When the minute hand points to **6**, we say **half past** the hour. The minute hand is *halfway* around the clock. The hour hand is *halfway* between the hour numbers.

The hour hand is halfway between **2** and **3**.
The minute hand points to **6**.

The time is **half past 2**, or **2:30**.

It is 30 minutes after 2.
It is **2:30**.

We can say: **"two thirty"**

Read the hour hand first. Then read the minute hand. Write the time.

1.

Half past ___4___

___4___:___30___

2.

Half past _____

_____:_____

3.

Half past _____

_____:_____

4.

Half past _____

_____:_____

5.

Half past _____

_____:_____

6.

Half past _____

_____:_____

Show Half Past

Draw hands on the clock and fill in the blanks to show the time.

1.

Half past ___8___

"__eight__ thirty"

8 : 30

2.

Half past _____

"_____ thirty"

6 : 30

3.

Half past _____

"twelve _____"

: 30

4.

Half past **5**

"_____ _____"

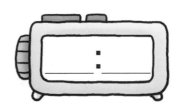

:

Telling Time

Write the time.

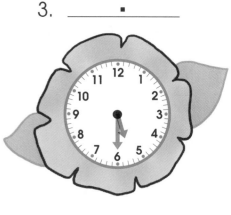

1. __1 : 30__

2. ___ : ___

3. ___ : ___

4. ___ : ___

5. ___ : ___

6. ___ : ___

Draw hands to show the time.

6:30

8:00

1:00

11:30

5:00

2:30

Earlier or Later

First, write the time or draw the hands in the **NOW** column.
Then, write the time for one hour earlier and one hour later.

One Hour Earlier	**NOW**	**One Hour Later**

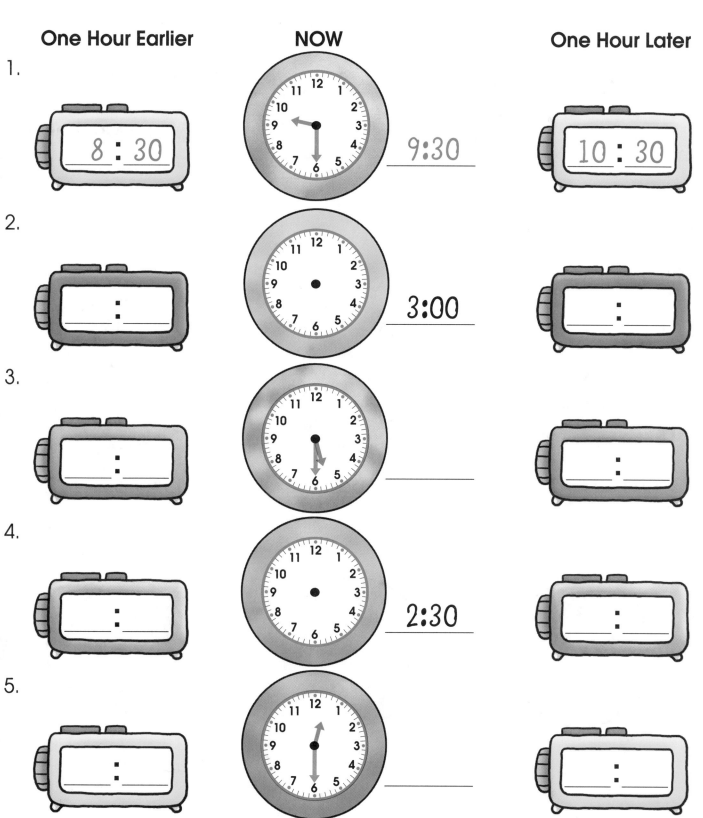

1. 8 : 30 — 9:30 — 10 : 30

2. ____ : ____ — 3:00 — ____ : ____

3. ____ : ____ — _____ — ____ : ____

4. ____ : ____ — 2:30 — ____ : ____

5. ____ : ____ — _____ — ____ : ____

Quarter Past the Hour

When the minute hand points to **3**, it is a quarter of the way around the clock. It is a **quarter past** the hour. The hour hand is a little past **2:00**.

The time is **quarter past 2**.

It is 15 minutes after 2.
It is **2:15**.

We can say: **"a quarter after 2"**

Read the hour hand first. Then read the minute hand.
Write the time.

1.

Quarter past ___6___

___6 : 15___

2.

Quarter past _____

___ : ___

3.

Quarter past _____

___ : ___

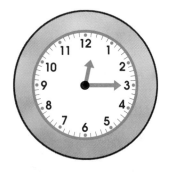

4.

Quarter past _____

___ : ___

5.

Quarter past _____

___ : ___

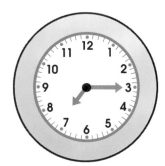

6.

Quarter past _____

___ : ___

Show Quarter Past

Draw hands on the clock and fill in the blanks to show the time.

1.

   Quarter past ___7___

   " _seven_ fifteen"

2.

   Quarter past **10**

   "_____ fifteen"

   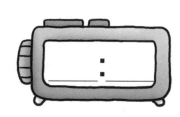

3.

   Quarter past _____

   "_____ fifteen"

4.

   Quarter past **3**

   "_____ _____"

   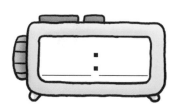

Quarter to the Hour

When the minute hand points to **9**, it is a **quarter to** the hour.
The hour hand is closer to the next hour.

The time is **quarter to 3**.
It is 15 minutes to 3.
We can say: **"a quarter to 3"**

OR

It is 45 minutes after 2.
It is **2:45**.
We can say: **"two forty-five"**

Read the hour hand first. Then read the minute hand.
Write the time.

1.

Quarter to _4_

_3_ : _45_

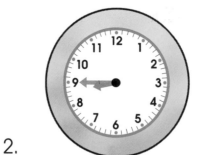

2.

Quarter to _____

___ : ___

3.

Quarter to _____

___ : ___

4.

Quarter to _____

___ : ___

5.

Quarter to _____

___ : ___

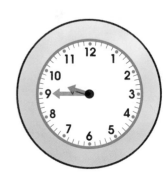

6.

Quarter to _____

___ : ___

Telling Quarter Hour Time

Write the time.

1. __1 : 45__

2. ___ : ___

3. ___ : ___

4. ___ : ___

5. ___ : ___

6. ___ : ___

Draw hands to show the time.

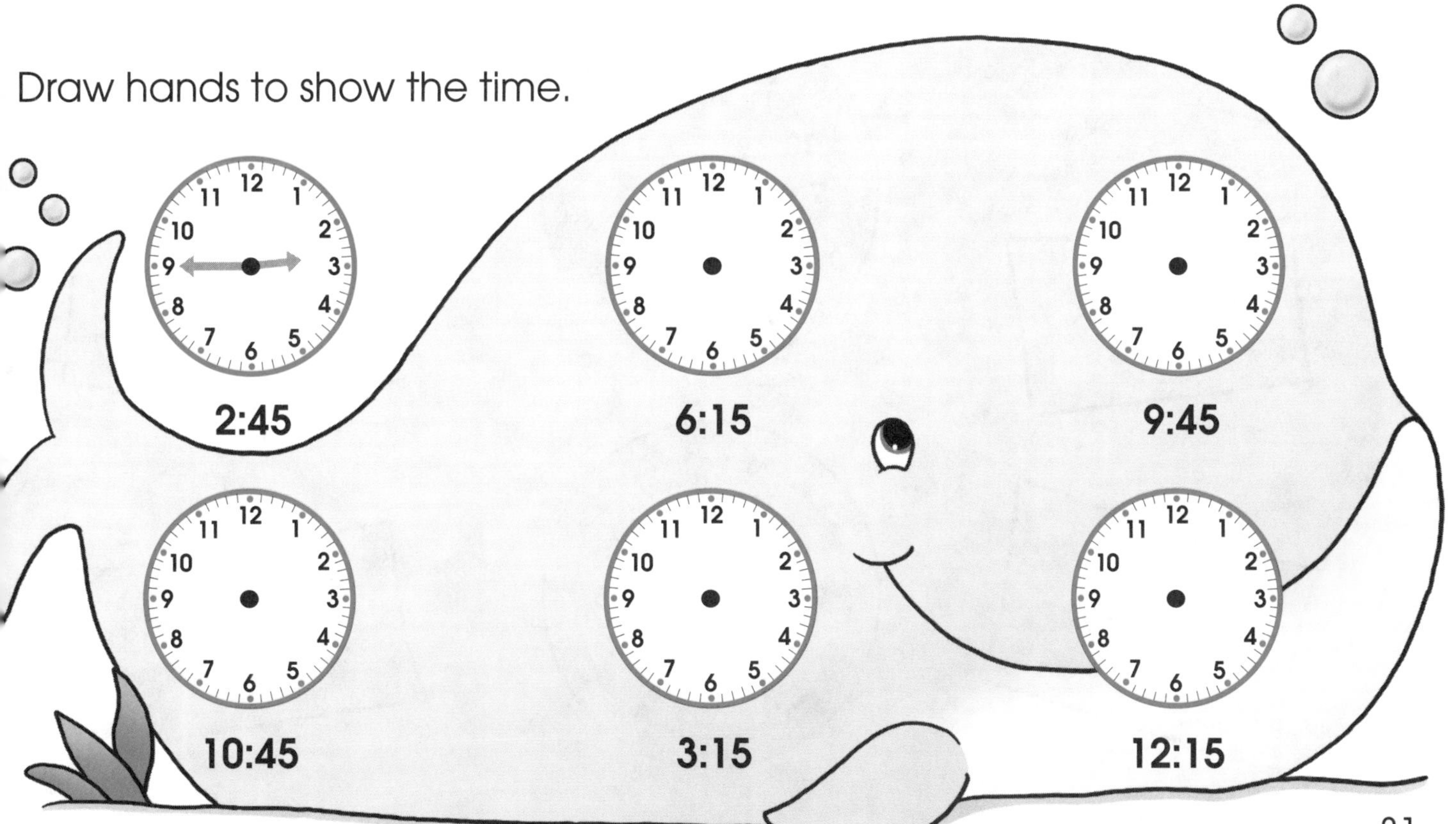

2:45

6:15

9:45

10:45

3:15

12:15

Match the Times

Match the time on the card to the clock. There is more than one card that matches each clock.

10:45

12:30

Quarter past 10

6:00

"ten forty-five"

10:15

6 o'clock

Half past 12

"ten fifteen"

Quarter to 11

Time Goes By

Draw hands to show the end time and write the end time.

Start Time	Amount of Time	End Time

1. **4:00** — The game is 3 hours long. — 7:00

2. **7:00** — The movie is 2 hours long. — __ : __

3. **11:30** — Lunch time is 30 minutes long. — __ : __

4. **8:30** — The school day is 6 hours long. — __ : __

5. **12:45** — The trip to the zoo is 4 hours long. — __ : __

Telling Time to Five Minutes

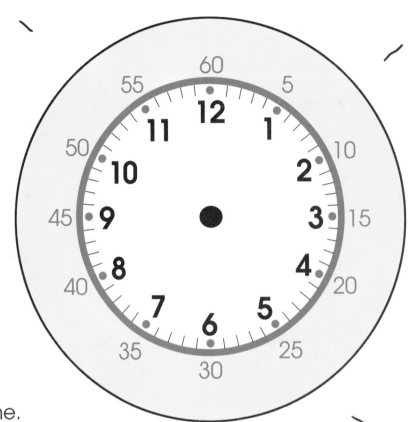

Write the time.

1. __4 : 05__

2. ____ : ____

3. ____ : ____

4. ____ : ____

5. ____ : ____

6. ____ : ____

Telling Time

Write the time.

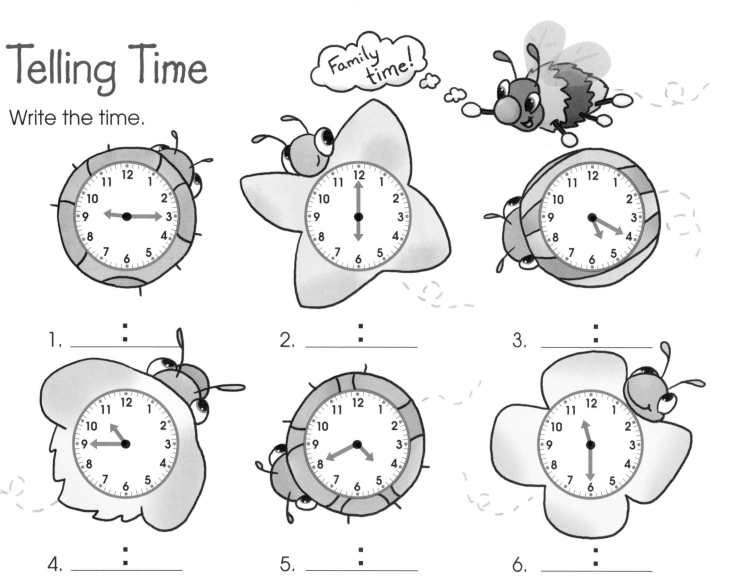

1. _____ : _____

2. _____ : _____

3. _____ : _____

4. _____ : _____

5. _____ : _____

6. _____ : _____

Draw hands to show the time.

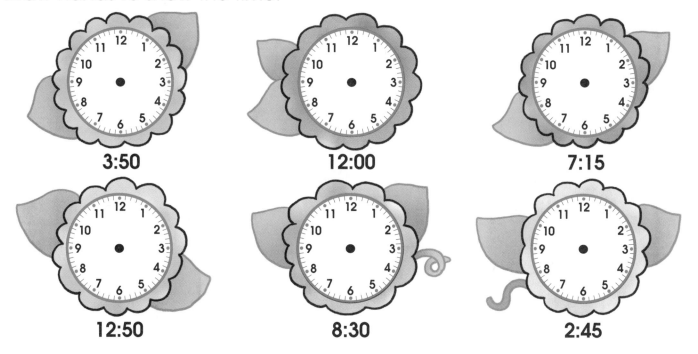

3:50

12:00

7:15

12:50

8:30

2:45

Find Equal Parts

Look at the shapes. One shape has 2 equal parts.

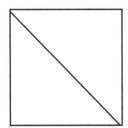
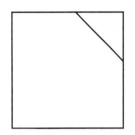

Equal Parts   Not Equal Parts

Circle the shapes that have equal parts.

1.
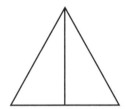

2.

3.
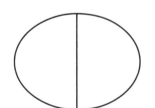

4.
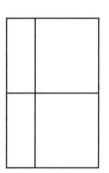
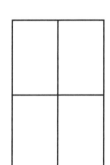

5.
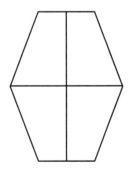
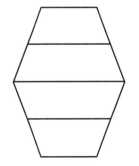

6.
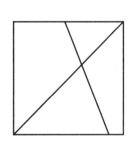
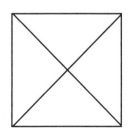

More Equal Parts

Look at the shapes. One shape has 4 equal parts.

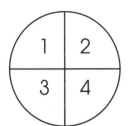 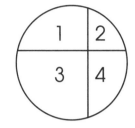

4 Equal Parts   4 Parts Not Equal

Circle the shapes that have equal parts.

1.

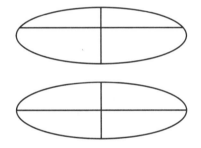

2.

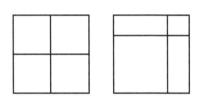

3.

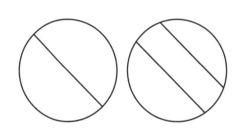

4.

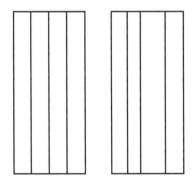

5.

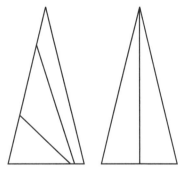

6.

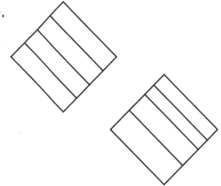

7.

8.

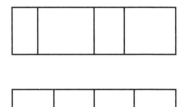

9.

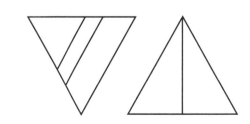

One-Half

Look at the shape. It has 2 equal parts. Each part is **one-half** or $\frac{1}{2}$.

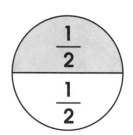

$\frac{1}{2}$ ← part colored
$\phantom{\frac{1}{2}}$ ← equal parts

$\frac{1}{2}$ is a **fraction**.

Write the fraction $\frac{1}{2}$ on each part.

1.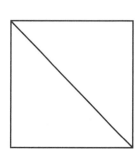

2.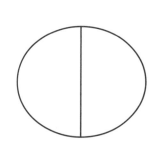

3.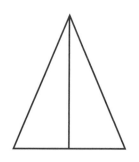

4.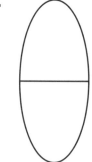

Color $\frac{1}{2}$ of each shape. The first one is done for you.

5.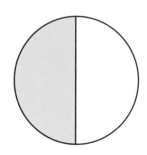

6.

7.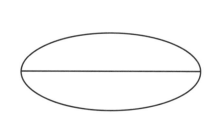

8.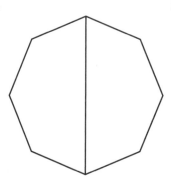

9.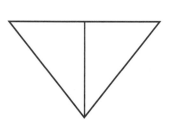

10.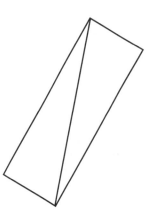

11.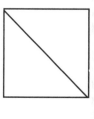

12.

Find One-Half

Mark an ✕ on the shapes that do not have 2 equal parts.
On the shapes without an ✕,
write $\frac{1}{2}$ on each part. Then color one of the parts.

1.

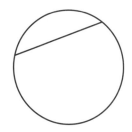

2.

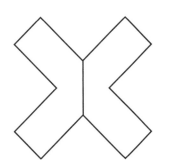

3.

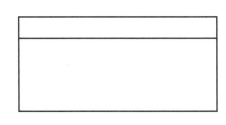

4.

5.

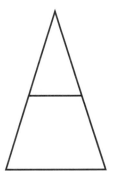

6.

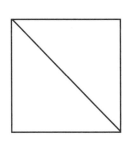

7.

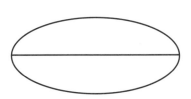

8.

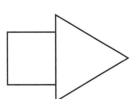

9.

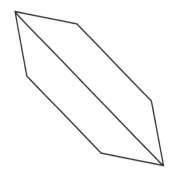

One-Third

Look at the shape. It has 3 equal parts. Each part is **one-third** or $\frac{1}{3}$.

$$\boxed{\frac{1}{3}} \quad \frac{1}{3} \quad \frac{1}{3}$$

$\frac{1}{3}$ ← part colored
$\frac{1}{3}$ ← equal parts

Write the fraction $\frac{1}{3}$ on each part.

1.

2.

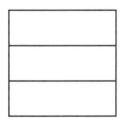

3.

4.

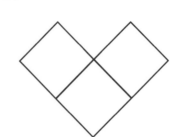

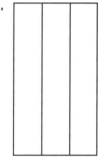

Color $\frac{1}{3}$ of each shape.

5.

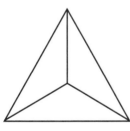

6.

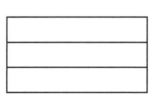

7.

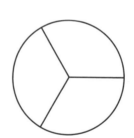

8.

9.

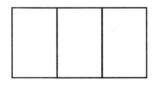

10.

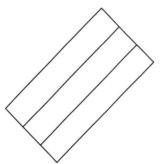

11.

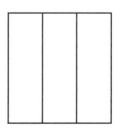

12.

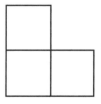

One-Fourth

Look at the shape. It has 4 equal parts. Each part is **one-fourth** or $\frac{1}{4}$.

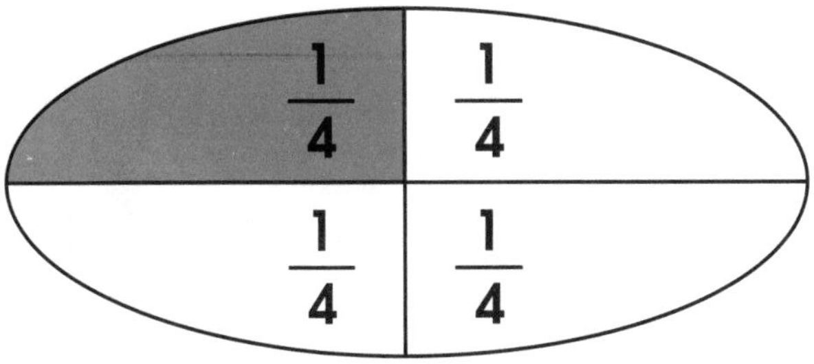

$\frac{1}{4}$ ← part colored / ← equal parts

Write the fraction $\frac{1}{4}$ on each part.

1.
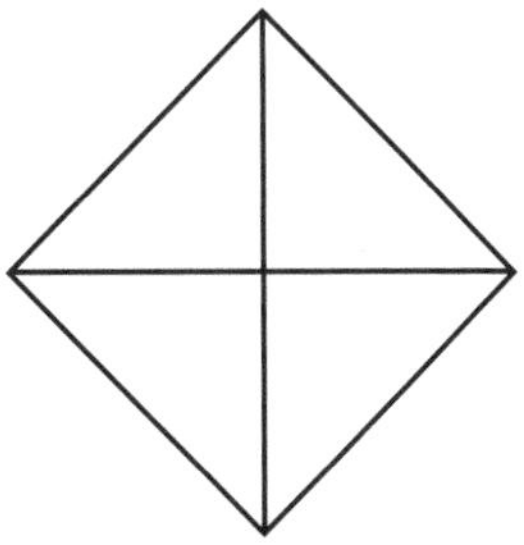

2.
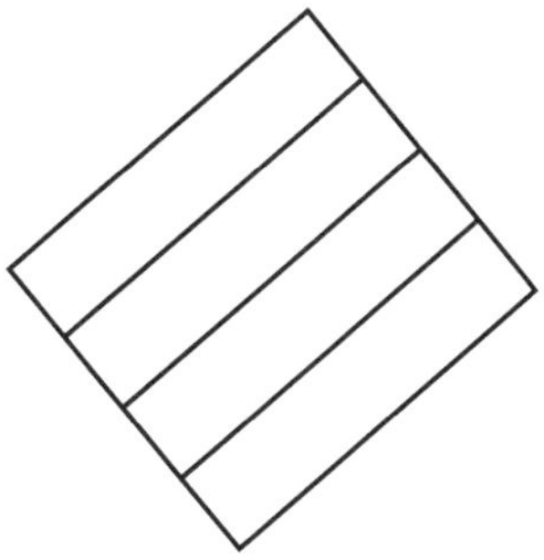

3.
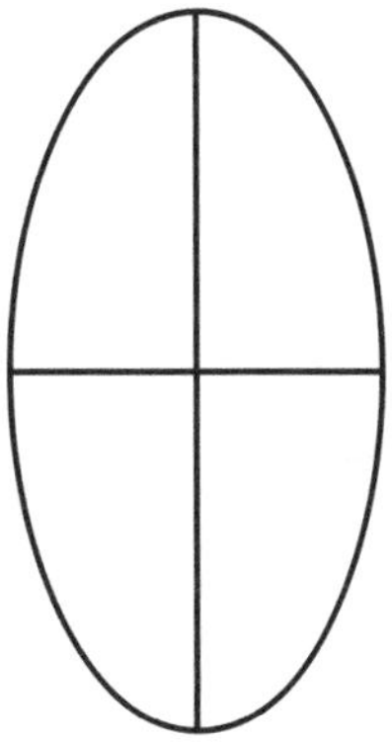

4.
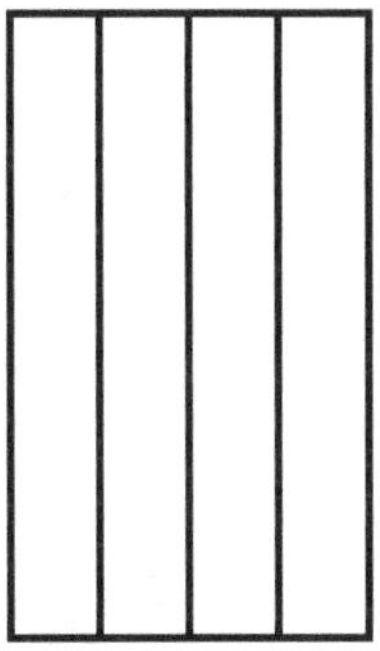

Color $\frac{1}{4}$ of each shape.

5.
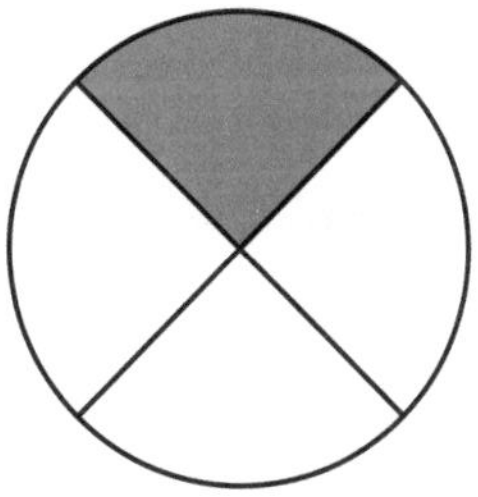

6.
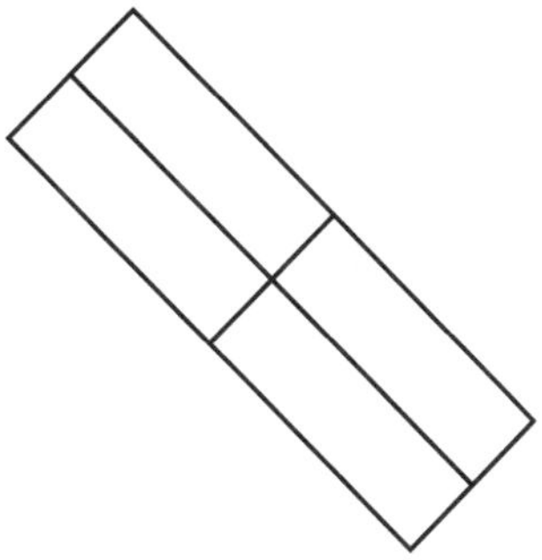

7.
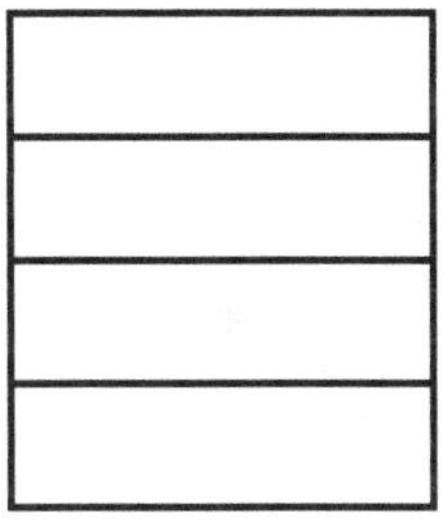

8.
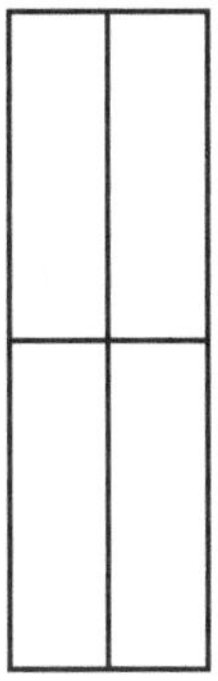

9.
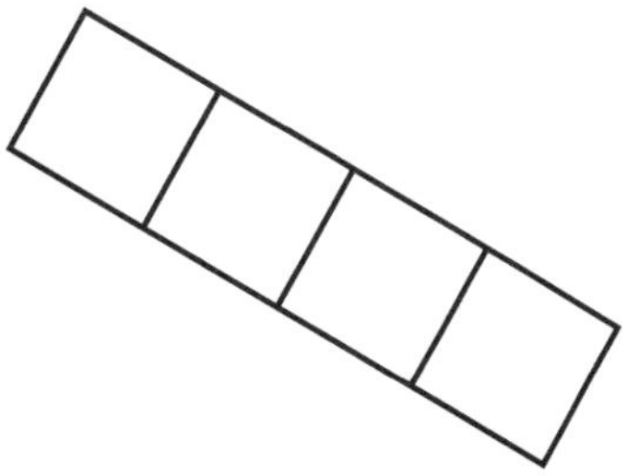

10.
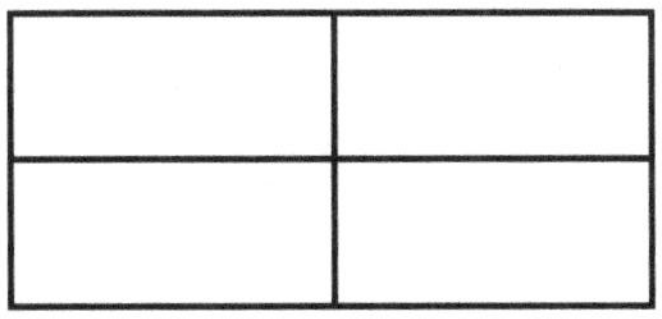

11.
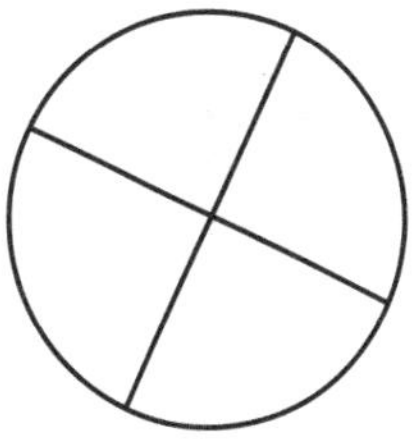

12.
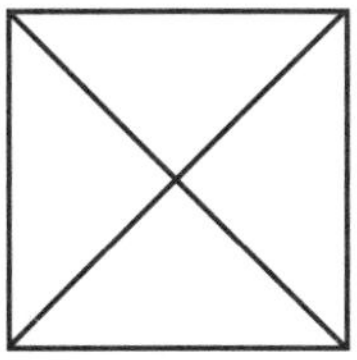

Name the Part

In a fraction, the top number tells how many parts are colored.
The bottom number of a fraction tells how many equal parts in all.

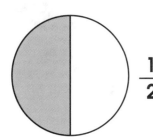 $\dfrac{1}{2}$ 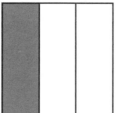 $\dfrac{1}{3}$ 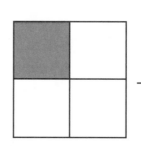 $\dfrac{1}{4}$

Write the fraction for the colored part of each shape.

1.

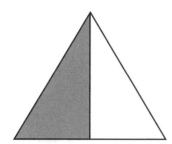 $\dfrac{1}{\boxed{2}}$

2.

 $\dfrac{\square}{3}$

3.

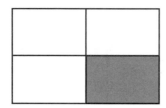 $\dfrac{\square}{\square}$

4.

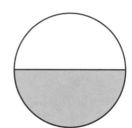 $\dfrac{\square}{\square}$

5.

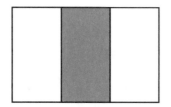 $\dfrac{\square}{\square}$

6.

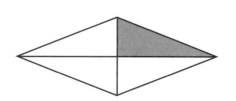 $\dfrac{\square}{\square}$

Pick the Fraction

Circle the correct fraction.

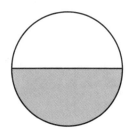

1. $\dfrac{1}{2}$ $\dfrac{1}{3}$ $\dfrac{1}{4}$

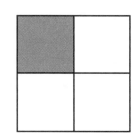

2. $\dfrac{1}{2}$ $\dfrac{1}{3}$ $\dfrac{1}{4}$

3. $\dfrac{1}{2}$ $\dfrac{1}{3}$ $\dfrac{1}{4}$

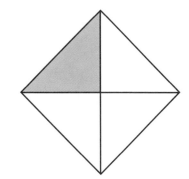

4. $\dfrac{1}{2}$ $\dfrac{1}{3}$ $\dfrac{1}{4}$

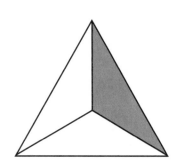

5. $\dfrac{1}{2}$ $\dfrac{1}{3}$ $\dfrac{1}{4}$

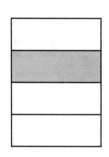

6. $\dfrac{1}{2}$ $\dfrac{1}{3}$ $\dfrac{1}{4}$

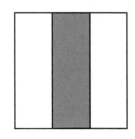

7. $\dfrac{1}{2}$ $\dfrac{1}{3}$ $\dfrac{1}{4}$

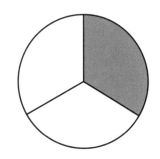

8. $\dfrac{1}{2}$ $\dfrac{1}{3}$ $\dfrac{1}{4}$

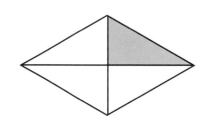

9. $\dfrac{1}{2}$ $\dfrac{1}{3}$ $\dfrac{1}{4}$

More Parts Colored

A fraction tells how many parts of a whole are being used.
These fractions tell about the colored parts of each shape.

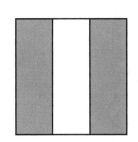

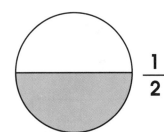
$\dfrac{1}{2}$

$\dfrac{2}{3}$ ←parts colored
←equal parts

$\dfrac{3}{4}$

Write the fraction to tell about the colored part of each shape.

1.

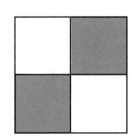
$\dfrac{2}{4}$

2.

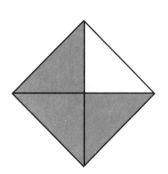
$\dfrac{3}{\boxed{}}$

3.

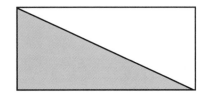
$\dfrac{\boxed{}}{\boxed{}}$

4.

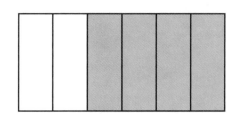
$\dfrac{\boxed{}}{\boxed{}}$

5.

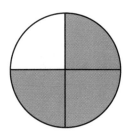
$\dfrac{\boxed{}}{\boxed{}}$

6.

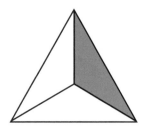

$\dfrac{\boxed{}}{\boxed{}}$

Pick the Fraction

Circle the correct fraction.

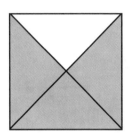

1. $\dfrac{3}{4}$ $\dfrac{1}{4}$ $\dfrac{2}{3}$

2. $\dfrac{2}{3}$ $\dfrac{1}{2}$ $\dfrac{1}{3}$

3. $\dfrac{1}{8}$ $\dfrac{7}{8}$ $\dfrac{3}{8}$

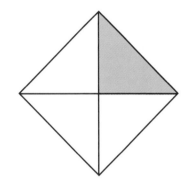

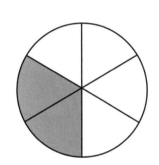

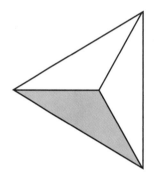

4. $\dfrac{1}{8}$ $\dfrac{2}{3}$ $\dfrac{1}{4}$

5. $\dfrac{1}{6}$ $\dfrac{1}{2}$ $\dfrac{2}{6}$

6. $\dfrac{1}{4}$ $\dfrac{1}{3}$ $\dfrac{1}{2}$

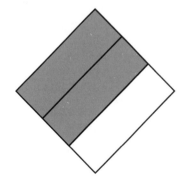

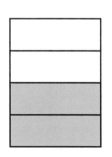

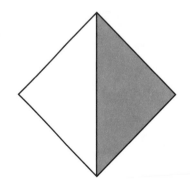

7. $\dfrac{1}{3}$ $\dfrac{2}{3}$ $\dfrac{1}{2}$

8. $\dfrac{3}{4}$ $\dfrac{1}{4}$ $\dfrac{2}{4}$

9. $\dfrac{1}{3}$ $\dfrac{1}{2}$ $\dfrac{2}{4}$

Show Fractional Parts

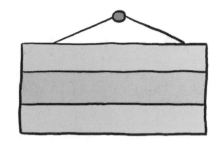

$\dfrac{2}{3}$ ← parts colored
← equal parts

Color the fractional part of the shape.

1. $\dfrac{1}{2}$

2. $\dfrac{2}{3}$

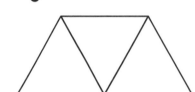

3. $\dfrac{4}{6}$

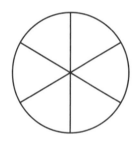

4. $\dfrac{1}{4}$

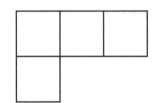

5. $\dfrac{5}{6}$

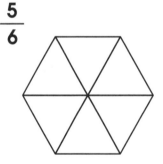

6. $\dfrac{3}{4}$

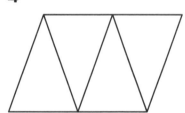

7. $\dfrac{3}{8}$

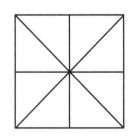

8. $\dfrac{2}{2}$

9. $\dfrac{2}{5}$

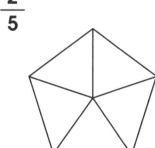

Draw Fractional Parts

Draw lines in the shape to show all the equal parts.
Then color the number of parts to show the fraction.

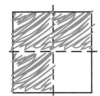 Look at the bottom number.
Draw 4 equal parts.

$$\frac{3}{4}$$

Look at the top number.
Color 3 of the parts.

Color the fractional part of the shape.

1. $\dfrac{1}{4}$

2. $\dfrac{1}{2}$

3. $\dfrac{2}{3}$

4. $\dfrac{1}{6}$

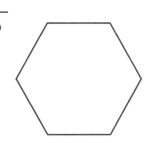

5. $\dfrac{3}{4}$

6. $\dfrac{2}{4}$

7. $\dfrac{3}{8}$

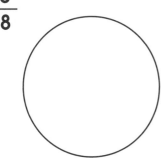

8. $\dfrac{4}{4}$

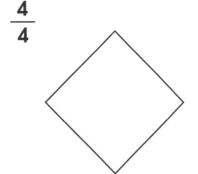

9. $\dfrac{7}{8}$

Fractional Part of a Group

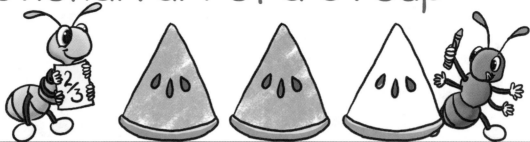

Color the objects to show the fraction.

1. $\dfrac{1}{2}$

2. $\dfrac{3}{4}$

3. $\dfrac{2}{3}$

4. $\dfrac{7}{8}$

5. $\dfrac{2}{5}$

6. $\dfrac{1}{4}$

7. $\dfrac{1}{8}$

8. $\dfrac{3}{6}$

More Fractional Parts

What fractional part of the group is green?

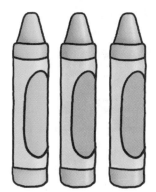

2 green crayons → **2**
3 crayons in all → **3**
_____
3

What part of each group is green? Write the fraction.

1. _3_
   4

2. **1**
   □

3. □
   □

4. □
   □
   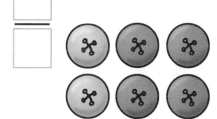

5. □
   □

6. □
   □
   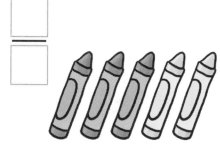

7. □
   □
   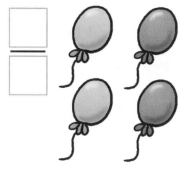

8. □
   □

9. □
   □

Half of a Group

The whole group is 4 cows.

$\frac{1}{2}$ $\frac{1}{2}$ Half of the group is 2 cows.

Circle half of the objects in each group.

1.

2.

3.

4.

5.

6.

Fractional Part of a Group

© School Zone Publishing Company

Show Fractional Parts

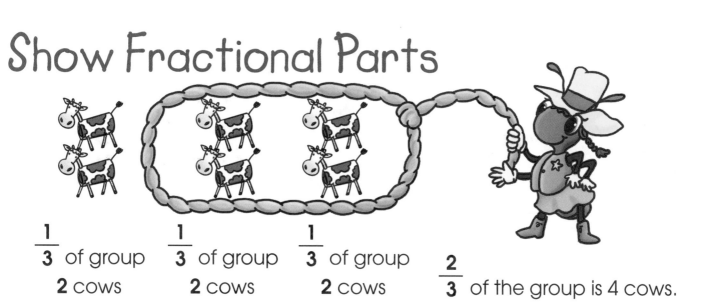

$\dfrac{1}{3}$ of group
2 cows

$\dfrac{1}{3}$ of group
2 cows

$\dfrac{1}{3}$ of group
2 cows

$\dfrac{2}{3}$ of the group is 4 cows.

Circle the objects to show the fractional part of the group.

1. $\dfrac{1}{3}$

2. $\dfrac{1}{4}$

3. $\dfrac{1}{4}$

4. $\dfrac{2}{3}$

5. $\dfrac{3}{4}$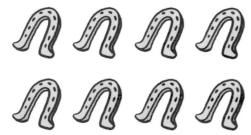

6. $\dfrac{2}{5}$

More About Fractions

 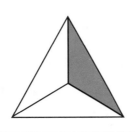 One-third $\dfrac{1}{3}$

Color the correct part of each shape or group.
Then write the fraction.

1. Color **one-fifth** of the shape.

2. Color **one-half** of the group.

3. Color **two-thirds** of the shape.

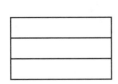 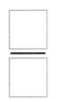

4. Color **three-fifths** of the group.

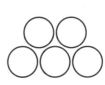

5. Color **three-fourths** of the shape.

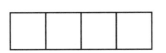

6. Color **four-sixths** of the group.

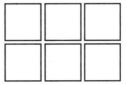

7. Color **one-half** of the shape.

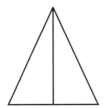 

8. Color **five-eighths** of the group.

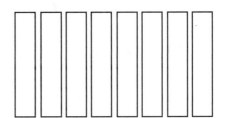 

Color Fractional Parts of Groups

Color the fractional parts of the objects in the picture.

1. Color $\frac{1}{2}$ of the shoes

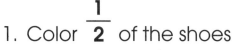 .

2. Color $\frac{2}{3}$ of the flowers

 .

3. Color $\frac{1}{3}$ of the stars

 .

4. Color $\frac{3}{5}$ of the balloons

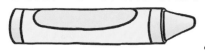 .

5. Color $\frac{5}{6}$ of the balls

 .

6. Color $\frac{1}{2}$ of the buttons

 .

7. Color $\frac{3}{4}$ of the bunnies

 .

What I Learned About Money

1. Count the money. Write the amount on the price tag.

_____ _____ _____ _____ _____ _____

2. Count the money. Is there enough to buy the item?

Yes

No

_____ _____ _____ _____ _____

3. Count the money. Write the amount.

¢ _____

4. Circle the fewest coins you need to buy this item.

Circle the correct answer.

5. Which coin has the same value as this group?

6. Count the money. What is the amount?

51¢   **76¢**   **81¢**

7. Count the money in groups A and B. Is the money in group A more, less, or equal to the amount in group B?

A.   B.

more   less   equal

8. Which coin is missing to make the amount?

9. What is the total amount for these 2 toys?

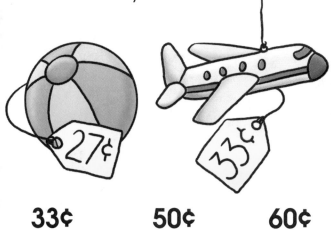

33¢   50¢   60¢

10. Find the amount of change.

Have   Buy   Change

$$35 ¢$$
$$-29 ¢$$

6¢   29¢   54¢

What I Learned About Time

Write the time in 2 ways.

1. _____ o'clock

_____ : _____

2. Half past _____

_____ : _____

3. Quarter to _____

_____ : _____

Draw hands on the clock face to show the time.

4. **5:30**

5. **11:00**

6. **7:15**

7. **12:20**

8. **5:45**

9. **1:50**

Circle the correct answer.

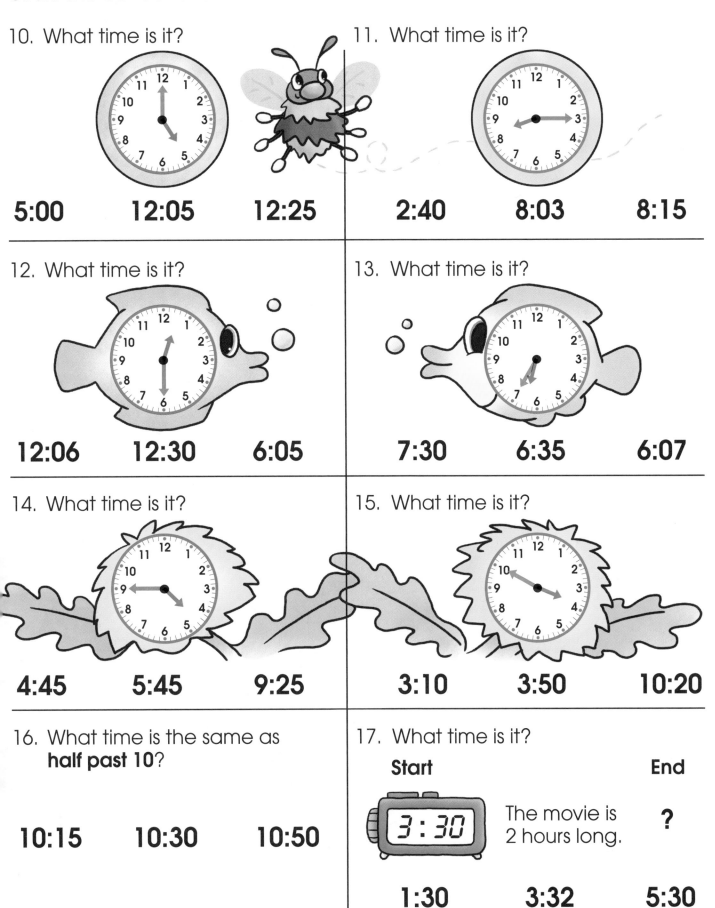

10. What time is it?

5:00   **12:05**   **12:25**

11. What time is it?

2:40   **8:03**   **8:15**

12. What time is it?

12:06   **12:30**   **6:05**

13. What time is it?

7:30   **6:35**   **6:07**

14. What time is it?

4:45   **5:45**   **9:25**

15. What time is it?

3:10   **3:50**   **10:20**

16. What time is the same as **half past 10**?

10:15   **10:30**   **10:50**

17. What time is it?

Start   **End**

The movie is 2 hours long.   **?**

1:30   **3:32**   **5:30**

What I Learned About Fractions

1. Circle the objects with equal parts.

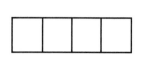   

Color the fractional part of the shape or group.

2. $\dfrac{1}{3}$

3. $\dfrac{1}{4}$

4. $\dfrac{5}{8}$

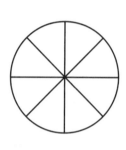

5. $\dfrac{2}{5}$

6. $\dfrac{3}{4}$

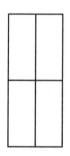

7. $\dfrac{1}{2}$

8. $\dfrac{5}{6}$

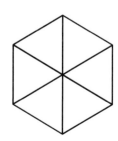

9. $\dfrac{2}{3}$

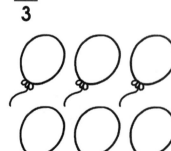

10. $\dfrac{6}{8}$

Look at the colored part of each shape or group.
Circle the correct answer.

11.

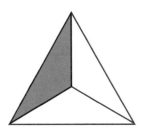

$\frac{1}{2}$ $\frac{1}{3}$ $\frac{1}{4}$

12.

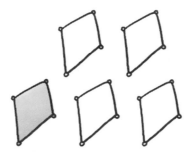

$\frac{1}{3}$ $\frac{1}{4}$ $\frac{1}{5}$

13.

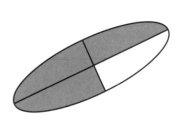

$\frac{1}{3}$ $\frac{3}{4}$ $\frac{1}{4}$

14.

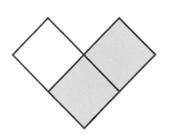

$\frac{1}{2}$ $\frac{1}{3}$ $\frac{2}{3}$

15.

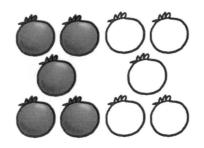

$\frac{1}{2}$ $\frac{1}{5}$ $\frac{5}{8}$

16.

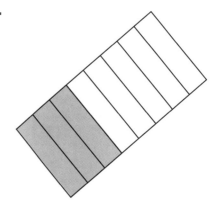

$\frac{1}{3}$ $\frac{3}{5}$ $\frac{3}{8}$

17.

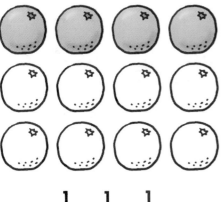

$\frac{1}{3}$ $\frac{1}{4}$ $\frac{1}{12}$

18.

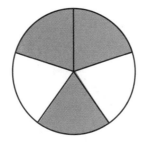

$\frac{2}{3}$ $\frac{2}{5}$ $\frac{3}{5}$

19.

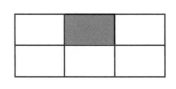

one-third

one-fifth

one-sixth

Answer Key

Page 1

1. 1, 2, 3, 4, 5, 6, 7 - 7¢
2. 5, 10, 15, 20, 25, 30 - 30¢
3. 10, 20, 30, 40, 50 - 50¢

Page 2

1. 10, 20, 30, 31, 32, 33, 34 - 34¢
2. 5, 10, 15, 20, 21, 22, 23 - 23¢
3. 10, 20, 30, 35, 40, 45, 50 - 50¢
4. 10, 20, 30, 40, 50, 51 - 51¢

Page 3

1. 10, 20, 30, 40, 50, 51, 52 - 52¢
2. 10, 20, 30, 35, 40, 41 - 41¢
3. 10, 15, 20, 21, 22, 23 - 23¢
4. 10, 20, 25, 30, 31 - 31¢

Page 4

1. 10¢
2. 33¢
3. 18¢
4. 25¢
5. 27¢
6. 36¢

Page 5

1. 36¢ glue
2. 33¢ paintbrush
3. 53¢ crayons
4. 30¢ pencils
5. 61¢ scissors
6. 46¢ notebook

Page 6

1. 25¢
2. 25¢
3. 28¢, crossed out
4. 25¢

Page 7

1. 36¢
2. 55¢
3. 76¢
4. 52¢
5. 87¢

Page 8

1. 25, 35, 45, 50, 51¢ Yes
2. 25, 50, 60, 65¢ No
3. 10, 20, 25, 30¢ Yes
4. 25, 50, 75, 76¢ Yes
5. 10, 20, 30, 31, 32¢ No

Page 9

1. 1 quarter, 1 dime, 3 pennies
2. 1 quarter, 2 dimes, 1 penny
3. 2 quarters, 1 dime, 2 nickels
4. 2 quarters, 2 nickels, 1 penny
5. 2 quarters, 2 pennies
6. 3 quarters, 1 dime, 2 pennies
Coin combinations can vary, please check your child's work.

Page 10

1. 1 quarter, 1 dime, 3 nickels
2. 3 dimes, 4 nickels
3. 1 quarter, 2 dimes, 1 nickel
4. 2 dimes, 4 nickels, 10 pennies

Page 11

1. 48¢
2. 50¢, circled
3. 50¢, circled
4. 60¢
5. 39¢
6. 50¢, circled

Page 12

1. 22¢, 31¢; eraser circled
2. 57¢, 52¢; scissors circled
3. 61¢, 60¢; whistle circled
4. 77¢, 82¢; notebook circled

Page 13

1. 25¢, 20¢; 20¢ circled
2. 50¢, 40¢; 40¢ circled
3. 35¢, 50¢; 35¢ circled
4. 50¢, 60¢; 50¢ circled
5. 75¢, 70¢; 70¢ circled
6. 60¢, 50¢; 50¢ circled
7. 70¢, 75¢; 70¢ circled
8. 75¢, 80¢; 75¢ circled

Page 14

1. D
2. D N
3. Q N P
4. Q D D P
5. Q P P

Page 15

1. Q N P P
2. Q P P P
3. Q D D
4. Q Q N P
5. Q Q D D
6. Q Q Q D D P P P

Page 16

1. 39¢
   + 28¢
   ———
   67¢

2. 44¢
   + 45¢
   ———
   89¢

3. 44¢
   + 17¢
   ———
   61¢

4. 36¢
   + 39¢
   ———
   75¢

5. 36¢
   + 45¢
   ———
   81¢

6. 17¢
   + 28¢
   ———
   45¢

Page 17

1. N 5¢
2. N P P P 8¢
3. D N 15¢
4. N P 6¢
5. D N P 16¢

Page 18

	Half Dollar	Quarter	Dime	Nickel	Penny
53¢	1				3
27¢		1			2
18¢			1	1	3
69¢	1		1	1	4
76¢	1	1			1
37¢		1	1		2
92¢	1	1	1	1	2

Answers can vary on the second table.

Page 19

Across	Down
a. 60	a. 62
b. 42	b. 45
c. 95	c. 90
d. 30	d. 35
e. 25	e. 25
f. 15	f. 10
g. 100	g. 10
h. 50	h. 55
i. 75	i. 74
j. 84	j. 89

Page 20

1. 2 o'clock
   2:00
2. 7 o'clock
   7:00
3. 9 o'clock
   9:00
4. 11 o'clock
   11:00
5. 8 o'clock
   8:00
6. 5 o'clock
   5:00

Page 21

1. 5:00
2.   10:00
3. 6:00
4. 12:00
5. 3:00
6.    8:00

Page 22

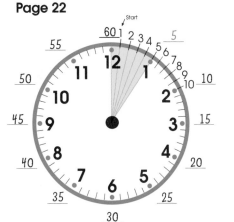

How many minutes in an hour? 60

Page 23

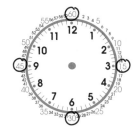

2. 5,10,15; 15 minutes
3. 5, 10, 15, 20, 25, 30;
   30 minutes
4. 5, 10, 15, 20, 25, 30,
   35, 40, 45; 45 minutes

Page 24

1. Half past 4
   4:30
2. Half past 10
   10:30
3. Half past 6
   6:30
4. Half past 8
   8:30
5. Half past 12
   12:30
6. Half past 3
   3:30

Page 25

1. Half past 8
   "eight thirty"   8:30
2. Half past 6
   " six thirty"   6:30
3. Half past 12
   "twelve thirty "   12:30
4. Half past 5
   " five thirty "   5:30

Page 26

1. 1:30   2. 6:00   3. 9:30
4. 10:30   5. 12:00   6. 5:30

6:30   8:00   1:00

11:30   5:00   2:30

Page 27

	One Hour Earlier	NOW	One Hour Later
1.	8 : 30	9:30	10 : 30
2.	2 : 00	3:00	4 : 00
3.	4 : 30	5:30	6 : 30
4.	1 : 30	2:30	3 : 30
5.	11 : 30	12:30	1 : 30

Page 28

1. Quarter past 6
   6:15
2. Quarter past 8
   8:15
3. Quarter past 1
   1:15
4. Quarter past 12
   12:15
5. Quarter past 10
   10:15
6. Quarter past 7
   7:15

Page 29

1. Quarter past 7
   " seven fifteen"   7:15
2. Quarter past 10
   " ten fifteen"   10:15
3. Quarter past 9
   " nine fifteen"   9:15
4. Quarter past 3
   " three fifteen"   3:15

Answer Key

Page 30

1. Quarter to 4
   3:45
2. Quarter to 9
   8:45
3. Quarter to 1
   12:45
4. Quarter to 7
   6:45
5. Quarter to 2
   1:45
6. Quarter to 10
   9:45

Page 31

1. 1:45 2. 2:15 3. 7:45
4. 11:15 5. 3:45 6. 8:15

 2:45
 6:15
 9:45

 10:45
 3:15
 12:15

Page 32

10:45   Quarter past 10   "ten forty-five"   6 o'clock   "ten fifteen"

12:30   6:00   10:15   Half past 12   Quarter to 11

Page 33

1.  7 : 00
2.  9 : 00
3.  12 : 00
4.  2 : 30
5.  4 : 45

Page 34

1. 4:05
2. 5:15
3. 3:10
4. 6:35
5. 9:50
6. 2:20

Page 35

1. 9:15 2. 6:00 3. 5:20
4. 10:45 5. 4:40 6. 11:30

 3:50
 12:00
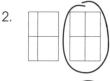 7:15

 12:50
 8:30
 2:45

Page 36

1.
2.
3.
4.
5.
6.

Page 37

1.
2.
3.
4.
5.
6.
7.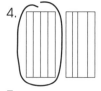
8.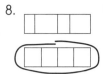
9.

Page 38

1.
| $\frac{1}{2}$ |
| $\frac{1}{2}$ |

2. $\frac{1}{2}$ $\frac{1}{2}$
3. 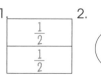 $\frac{1}{2}$ $\frac{1}{2}$
4. 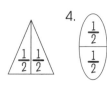 $\frac{1}{2}$ $\frac{1}{2}$

5.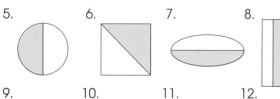
6.
7.
8.

9.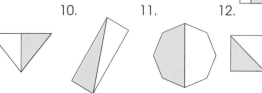
10.
11.
12.

The $\frac{1}{2}$ section colored can vary.

Page 39

1.
2.
3.

4.
5.
6.

7.
8.
9.

The $\frac{1}{2}$ section colored can vary.

Page 40

1.
2.
3.
4.

5.
6.
7.
8.

9.
10.
11.
12.

The $\frac{1}{3}$ section colored can vary.

Page 41

1.
2.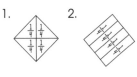
3.
4.

5.
6.
7.
8.

9.
10.
11.
12.

The $\frac{1}{4}$ section colored can vary.

Page 42

1. 1/2
2. 1/3
3. 1/4
4. 1/2
5. 1/3
6. 1/4

Page 43

1. 1/2
2. 1/4
3. 1/3
4. 1/4
5. 1/3
6. 1/4
7. 1/3
8. 1/3
9. 1/4

Page 44

1. 2/4
2. 3/4
3. 1/2
4. 4/6
5. 3/4
6. 1/3

Page 45

1. 3/4
2. 1/3
3. 3/8
4. 1/4
5. 2/6
6. 1/3
7. 2/3
8. 2/4
9. 1/2

Page 47

1. $\frac{1}{4}$
2. $\frac{1}{2}$
3. $\frac{2}{3}$

4. $\frac{1}{6}$
5. $\frac{3}{4}$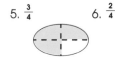
6. $\frac{2}{4}$

7. $\frac{3}{8}$
8. $\frac{4}{4}$
9. $\frac{7}{8}$

Sections colored can vary,
please check your child's work.

Page 46

1. $\frac{1}{2}$
2. $\frac{2}{3}$
3. $\frac{4}{6}$

4. $\frac{1}{4}$
5. $\frac{5}{6}$
6. $\frac{3}{4}$

7. $\frac{3}{8}$
8. $\frac{2}{2}$
9. $\frac{2}{5}$

Sections colored can vary,
please check your child's work.

Page 48

1. one is colored
2. three are colored
3. two are colored
4. seven are colored
5. two are colored
6. one is colored
7. one is colored
8. three are colored

Page 49

1. 3/4
2. 1/3
3. 1/2
4. 2/6
5. 1/4
6. 3/5
7. 2/4
8. 4/8
9. 3/3

Page 50

1.
2.

3.
4.

5.
6.

Objects circled can vary,
please check your child's work.

Answer Key

Page 51

1. $\frac{1}{3}$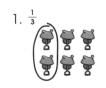

2. $\frac{1}{4}$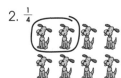

3. $\frac{1}{4}$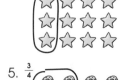

4. $\frac{2}{3}$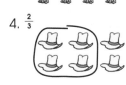

5. $\frac{3}{4}$

6. $\frac{2}{5}$

Objects circled can vary, please check your child's work.

Page 52

1. $\boxed{\frac{1}{5}}$

2. $\boxed{\frac{1}{2}}$

3. $\boxed{\frac{2}{3}}$

4. $\boxed{\frac{3}{5}}$

5. $\boxed{\frac{3}{4}}$

6. $\boxed{\frac{4}{6}}$

7. $\boxed{\frac{1}{2}}$

8. $\boxed{\frac{5}{8}}$

Sections colored can vary, please check your child's work.

Page 53

Objects colored can vary, please check you[r] child's work.

Pages 54–55

1. 10, 20, 25, 26, 27, 28; 28¢
2. 25, 50, 60, 65, 66¢; No
3. 92¢
4. 1 half dollar, 2 dimes, 2 pennies
5. half dollar
6. 76¢
7. more
8. nickel
9. 60¢
10. 6¢

Pages 56–57

1. 8 o'clock, 8:00
2. Half past 11, 11:30
3. Quarter to 2, 1:45

4. 5. 6.
7. 8. 9.

10. 5:00   11. 8:15
12. 12:30 13. 6:35
14. 4:45   15. 3:50
16. 10:30 17. 5:30

11. 1/3   12. 1/5
13. 3/4   14. 2/3
15. 1/2   16. 3/8
17. 1/3   18. 3/5
19. one-sixth

Pages 58–59

1.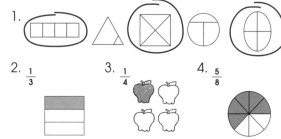

2. $\frac{1}{3}$

3. $\frac{1}{4}$

4. $\frac{5}{8}$

5. $\frac{2}{5}$

6. $\frac{3}{4}$

7. $\frac{1}{2}$

8. $\frac{5}{6}$

9. $\frac{2}{3}$

10. $\frac{6}{8}$

Sections colored can vary, please check your child's work.

Time, Money & Fractions, Grade 1–2 **02211**